Catching Light

Catching Light

Published by Poetry Space Ltd. 2013

©2013 Margaret Eddershaw

Edited by Wendy French

Design and layout Susan Jane Sims

Cover Photograph © Eleanor Bennett

All rights reserved.
No part of this book may be reproduced or transmitted in any form or by any means without written permission of the publisher. Individual copyright remains with the poet.

This edition first published in Great Britain in 2013 by Poetry Space Ltd.

Poetry Space Ltd. Company No. 7144469.
All rights reserved.
Reg.office. 21 Davis Close, Barrs Court, Bristol, BS30 7BU

Printed and Bound in Great Britain
by Inky Little Fingers Ltd

ISBN 978-1-909404-08-3

www.poetryspace.co.uk

Catching Light

by Margaret Eddershaw

For 25 years Margaret Eddershaw was an actor, director and university teacher of theatre. She has published on Brecht, Stanislavski, and theatre history. She performed three of her own one-woman plays at the Edinburgh Fringe Festival, on tour and in London during the 1980s.

In 1995, she took up residence in Greece and began writing poems. Since then, she has had over 150 published in magazines and anthologies, and given readings in Athens and London.

Between 2008 and 2012, Margaret wrote four suites of performance poems and presented them at Chester and Lancaster Literature Festivals, and various venues in Manchester, London and Helsinki.

This is her first full poetry collection.

For Keith

CONTENTS

I : BRIEF ENCOUNTERS

The Hat	10
San Story	11
Marine	12
Beggar	13
Marilyn's No.1 Fan	14
Washing-Line	15
Piranha	16
Bare Bones	17
Salvador Solution	18
His New Shoes	19
Getting Old	20
Kurd	21
She Can't Speak	22
Choosing the *Tagelmoust*	23
Waiting	24
Bosom Friends	25
Pierced Ears	26
Like George	27
Pompeii Potter	28
Visit	29

II : HOME THOUGHTS

Second Homing	31
Barmaid	32
Navigating the Night	33
Stay Indoors	34
Copycat	35
Healing Hat	36
Sprouts	37
Rare Orchid	38
On Porpoise	39

Falling Star	40
Mickey v Minnie	41
Burning Primrose	42
Dead Sister's Gloves	43
Solstice	44
Alive, Alive, Oh!	45
Afghan Coat	46
Matter	47
First Ballet Dress	48
Fall of a Sparrow	49
Golden Rule	50

III : TRAVELLER TALES

In the Mist	52
Comet Over Lesotho	53
To the Camel	54
Amazon Green	55
Visiting LA	56
Driving Through Butterflies	57
Caretta Caretta	58
At the Fleadh	59
Downstream	60
Whales at Hermanus	61
Sandstorm	62
Feet of Clay	63
Glacier	64
Tigerhunt	65
Knitting Ensemble	66
Prisoner 46664	67
Frigate Bird	68
At Ghandi's Monument	69
Township School	70
Desert Dance	71

Acknowledgements are due to:

Aabye, Aspire, Barnet Anthology, Beehive Poetry, Carillon, Cinnamon Press, Earlyworks Press, First Time, Interpreter's House, Iota, King's Lynn Festival Anthology, Krax, Lancaster Litfest Anthology, Loose Muse Anthology, Margaret Munro Anthology, Mere Literary Festival Anthology, Ouse Valley Poetry, Partners in Poetry, Pennine Platform, Poetry Monthly, Poetry Space, Purple Patch, Quantum Leap, Robooth Publications, Segora, Speakeasy Poets, Ver Poets, Wells Literature Festival.

I : BRIEF ENCOUNTERS

THE HAT

I could swear the dog
sometimes wore the hat -
cheeky, porkpie number
angled for flight
whereas the body

both bodies, rotund
earthbound, swayed
on cabriole legs
buttocks wobbling
in unison.

But the dog never wore the glasses.
I remember the man
peering at distorted trees,
side by side in the park
he on the bench-end
dog hunkered by trouser-leg
pale bellies matched.

Today
the man sits alone
ghost of a lead in his hand
hatless.

SAN STORY

Somehow the photo of them
came out black and white.
Their village was moved three days' walk
from this ancient ground,
but five young men stayed
to share with tourists
their sense of desert
beneath the skin,
how they inhale the warm mind
of hidden prey –
snapshots of a dwindled life
exploiting
the Kalahari's meagring resources.

We follow in their bare footsteps,
behind soft wraps of kudu hide
and slant sticks,
as they finger plants for healing,
hold one wing of an insect delicious to eat,
take turns to enact tribal stories
with precise gestures,
San sounds tumbling out,
punctuated by rapid clicks of tongue,
a river rushing over pebbles.

The star performer plays a hunter
who kills an ant-eater,
then cuts open its stomach,
returning the still live ants within,
to the ant-hill.

And as the men leave,
straight-spined
balanced,
their lively colours
fade to black and white.

MARINE

The toes of his boots,
tough as the wearer,
turned skywards
to mirror the raptor's nose
suspended
over the metal chin-strap
of his Royal Marine cap.

He was in civvies that day,
when his impatience with a non-swimmer
made him hurl the five year old
into a bone-chilling sea,
off the shingled, Sussex coast -
until choking
flailing limbs
serious sinking
forced him to save his drowning niece.

For thirty years, swirling water
filled her nightmare ears
froze her lungs within their cage
as she stood at briny edges.

Till a sea-change:
the silky Mediterranean
warm as bath-water
coaxed her into floating
then swimming sure as a new-born turtle.
Tell that to the Marines.

BEGGAR

Bright cloth winds
her old-child face,
dense layers
hang sorrowfully
from a gaunt frame.

Bird beady eyes flicker
into anxious corners,
lips shape mutters,
two coins shining
on a calloused palm
underline the meaning.

Fumbling for my purse
I see her curled feet
thrust into sandals
too small
one heel broken
a pair I threw away yesterday.

Her feet shuffle
under my gaze
and I wonder how she feels
in my shoes.

MARILYN'S No.1 FAN

That light breathy voice sings
Happy Birthday to you -
lookalike girls teeter on high heels
flutter eyelashes under blonde wigs.

Through the excited crowd
in a dandruffed suit
weighed down with badges
brooches, fan-club pins
and promotional tags,
he weaves towards me.

That lass stars at my house
every night of the week.
We have dinner together
me at one end of the table
she at t'other. I toast her
and she smiles at me.

At my sceptical look -
She's a life-size cut-out
nicked from a Salford cinema
February 14, 1958.

After dinner
I take her upstairs -
her room's wallpapered
with photos and posters.

They tease me at work
but I don't care.

WASHING-LINE

Something odd about them
from the beginning
not just British reserve -
we never heard them speak -
and the washing-line clinched it.

Each morning of their week's vacation
a long row of pure white underwear
plain, thick cotton
his and hers
alternating
perfectly pegged.

Yet minutely re-organised during drying:
he appeared
squeezed a peg one centimetre right
then she came
eased a bra to the left.

No other garments
each day ghostly undies
paraded their obedient souls
with military precision,
barely raising a flutter of life.

PIRANHA

Our canoe noses lazy reeds
glides between liana snakes
into an emerald cavern
of half-drowned trees
perfectly reflected in tea-stain water.

Warm raindrops patter
onto concentric circles
fallen blossoms swirl around the hull
cocooning us
in a giant bead of perspiration.

Then bamboo rods beat the surface
to lure fish.

A piranha dangles
whiplashes air
growls when I unhook it
somersaults between my feet
petrol blue sides heave
eyes bulge
gasps force open
a circular saw of teeth.

When the speedboat struck
threw us into the fast-running Amazon
and we choked for breath
clinging to our overturned canoe
I thought of that fish.

BARE BONES

Old part of town,
new foundations
discover a grave,
unseen for centuries.

An image of serenity:
her wrists crossed,
finger bones splayed on chest,
twists of rotted thread
fallen.

Amphora - earth-filled now -
deliberately placed
beside each white hip,
ritual certainty
among the throb of traffic.

She's calm in the face
of arguing professionals,
team-leader shrill in power suit,
expansive gestures
deriding others' incompetence,

as the bones are transferred,
without ceremony,
to plastic supermarket bags.

SALVADOR SOLUTION

The carnival narcotic
pulses Brazilian veins
red corpuscles flow
seeming aimless
in a flood of flesh
throbbing the streets.

White corpuscles thrust
against the tide's
inevitable currents
each squad of riot police
warns of tourists stripped
in this infested river.

Then the beat takes over
our bodies begin to sway
shimmy between dancers
stop to samba with a stranger
re-join the bloodstream
its circulation carries us home.

HIS NEW SHOES

Polished toe-caps
like a pair of black ears
listening for his heartbeat
push through the carnation coverlet
that climbs to meet waxy fingers.
A whisper of commiseration
wafts in a newcomer to join
the circle of kindly crows.
My eye follows the lace
round the coffin back to the shoes.

Too small, aren't they?
Did they break his toes?

Long sighs shiver
the surface of bitter coffee,
a persistent fly
knowing more than we admit
is waved from his face.

Maybe the shoes are false,
undertakers' props?

We wait
for Lazarus to perform his trick
stand up in his new shoes
slide like a boy on shiny soles.

A gaunt profile tumbles into tears
condemning our dry cheeks.
Then the priest shuffles past fat knees.
Panicked by holy gestures
the fly embarks on a journey
around the new shoes.

GETTING OLD

To tell you the truth,
she whispered,
*There's nothing to be said
for getting old.*

What about wisdom, grace, peace?
I asked.

It's all about loss,
she said,
*Loss of teeth, hair, sight and breath,
loss of balance,
purpose
and reason.*

And absence?
I enquired.

*Yes, a permanent absence
of friends,*
she replied.

KURD

Elegant fingers serve apple-tea
hollowed face hovers
dangerously distinct
in Istanbul.

Stranger, too, in the east
his own ancient land
Mesopotamia
a people between rivers
of winter tears
caught in contrary currents
leaching red.

As I sip my tea
he recalls his lost home
beautiful
fruitful
discomforts forgotten.

SHE CAN'T SPEAK

Drama will be good for her, they said
challenging me to break and enter.
She's twenty-five, they said.
Autistic, they said.

I thought:
By what right do I presume
to know better?
Is it normal to see extreme poverty
starvation
killing
and go on living?

Why not leave Janet in her world
driven by a comforting spiral of paper
expertly spun before intense eyes?

She can't make decisions, they said.
Each week with me
she decides
to shrink from my touch
to sit while others move
to scowl instead of smile.

Then after a life without words
she decides to speak -
No, she said.

CHOOSING THE *TAGELMOUST*
(a Touareg headdress)

turban
hiding all but shades
bends beside me
with sapphire

dark jelabia throws
midnight blue
over my shoulder

long brown fingers
with agate ring
hold aquamarine
to my cheek -
they want to match my eyes

rapid Arabic
laughter with mint-tea breath
slapping of pale palms
and sleeves stretch to measure

ringed hand drapes the chosen cloth
over my crown
a length free on one side
folds a loop below the chin
wraps the width behind my head
across the brow
twists for tension
winds round twice more
tucks in the end

bearded voice says:
English lady ready Sahara

WAITING

A restless humbug of zebras
gathers among trees
they pass a near gap in the brush
become barcodes on a lioness's shopping.

I hunker at the waterhole
concealed in sere grass
tail curling haunches
amber eyes half-closed.

Their ears rotate like aerials
above bulging bellies
hooves slip at the water's edge
my claws squeeze forward
back legs tense
eyes wide at this black and white movie.

One muzzle lifts at a whiff of enemy
he skitters away
spooking the rest.
I smile.

Thirst leads a female back
brown foal nosing her rear
I fix on the tender prey
my black-tipped tail flickers
but zebra heads jostle
obscuring my line of attack
they suck urgent water
as far as scrubbing-brush manes
I remain in the moment.

BOSOM FRIENDS

From Saigon's bright bustling
into an Aladdin's cave,
shelves of silk in strata
of sapphire, emerald, ruby.

She flows soft rivers through her arms,
across the rush-matted floor
over my shoulders
hands dancing
framing me with chosen fabric.

Sweat sequins her brow
jet eyes twinkle beside
an ebony fall of hair.
A bonsai woman with twiglike arms
tiny trunk, swaying
in an imperceptible breeze
slim legs
two downward strokes
of a calligrapher's brush.
I dwarf her.

She clambers onto a stool
calling figures to an assistant,
passes the tape around me
across my bust - looks at the number
hesitates
checks.
Our eyes meet -
words rustling like leaves
she says, *Nice big titties!*
cups them in miniature fingers.
I'd rather be your size, I reply
and we laugh and hug.

PIERCED EARS

Her energy lit the carriage
despite the grind of wheels
dragging us to London Bridge,
her beam engulfed me.
Seventy-five, she said,
hubby recently deceased,
now she was released
in a manner of speaking
to do things she never had:

go abroad on holiday
re-decorate the bathroom
see a West End musical
have her ears pierced
(the latter already done
proof dangled jauntily)
a mystery why she waited
greater choice of earrings
no more pinched lobes
on nights out.

Her high octane chatter a delight,
her grabbing at life
with both plump fists,
inspiring.
I gave her my Greek address.
And the next day
had my ears pierced.

LIKE GEORGE

In a bar at Alice Springs
he held me with a glittering eye.
From behind a lopsided smile
past a slurring tongue
What do I look like? asked George.

The stone-age brow
of an Australian aborigine
loured over grey eyes
native to the Andes.
What do I look like? he repeated.

Flared nostrils aligned him
to the African bushman
full lips to the Innuit,
glossy black hair to the Red Indian.
"What manner of man art thou?" I thought.

One uncivilised by civilization
despised for alternative myths
caught like a fly in amber
between then and now.
I'm only half abo but I can track, he said.

His face had the dull lustre
of a black Pacific pearl
rare yet less valued than
the ubiquitous pale kind.
And I'm half Greek gyppo, he added.

The flightless cassowary
could not explain this creation
and white man's firewater
left him dreaming on the edge.
But I <u>am</u> an Australian, aren't I? asked George

POMPEII POTTER

August hotter than usual
flies, haze
even cicadas weary.
Then reek of sulphur
a few tremors
umbrella cloud at the peak
flames in the night.

But many orders to fill.
Early morning
ash drifts onto spinning clay
like snow
like old skin
like long sighs.

A stronger quake shivers walls
throws pots from a shelf.
Large rim to hand-smooth
storage jar for firing.

Sudden ricochets on the roof
screams
running
burning pumice bounces down the street
furnace-like heat -

He squats on among his wares
hands clenched to face
flesh atomised in Vesuvius' kiln
bodily space entombed in tufa
last thoughts
dust.

VISIT

A child tied to her back
in a checked shawl,
she leads us
with a wide-hipped sway
past other grandchildren,
fussing like chickens,
to a circle of thatched huts.

The blackened kitchen
reels with smoke,
ash drifting over neat pots.

Furniture crowds the living space,
on its mud-brick wall
a framed certificate
for long railway service.

One hut has frayed bedrolls
well-stowed,
a rough table for homework.

Leaning on each other
in the store,
two lone sacks of grain,
to feed the family of nine
for six months.

With the serene smile
of a society hostess, she asks:
When is the Queen coming to visit?

II : HOME THOUGHTS

SECOND HOMING

As I leave like a treacherous swallow,
homing pigeons chorus their disapproval.
What's wrong with Britain? they cluck.
My freedom slams the door of their coop,
sows seeds of doubt in the abandoned soil.

The lure of otherness tempts a cuckoo
to make a foreign nest its own.
Aren't you burning your boats? they croak.
My past has not turned to ashes,
but its first cycle is rounded like a dream.

Why live in Greece? they coo.
Is it not enough for mountains to recede
in immeasurable layers of blue,
to watch the gaudy dance of oranges
in open-skied Novembers?

But you'll be a foreigner there, they chirrup,
not knowing the flowing easiness here
that expands the inner space for self.
I unfurl like a rare flower in generous light
that defines me by more than ethnicity.

What about Christmas? they twitter.
Here where the cradle of western theatre
rocks to the music of every heart,
my sun-steeped, ageing bones
already sense a real belonging.
And they squawk: *Shall we send you Marmite?*

BARMAID

In an alien world
of thick laughter
blasts of pop
raucous shouts
metallic throb of slot-machine
empty bottles crated,
thud of darts
click of beer-tops
and tills rattling,
the bright butterfly
is pinned behind the bar.

Weary eyes flickering
toward the slow moving clock,
she flutters between customers,
caught in a draught of rising tempers,
scoured by dozens of glazed eyes,
flayed by flabby fingers
grasping change.

She smiles at leers
winks
smutty remarks
tall tales of woe, women, wine consumed
and cries of *What's yours, darling?*
until the bell signals release
and she can wriggle free.

NAVIGATING THE NIGHT

Waking in the small hours
sleep as slippery as a shoal
he re-lives his old routine:
leaving home before stars fade
crunch of shingle under waders
father loading fish-boxes
brother checking the engine
granddad greasing winches
quick sips of thermos tea
before the clinker-strong trawler
glides between groynes
ploughs over grey surge.

Bow nosing toward the horizon
his night's eye checks compass points
store-boxes moored close in
lobster-pots on buoys out further
then his sea-chart memory unfurls
deep water constellations
crevasses scoring chalk reefs
a shipwreck tilted on seabed pebbles
massive sandstone clusters
marking the moment to pay out nets
till the swell and rock of his bed
haul sleep aboard once more.

STAY INDOORS

In your fifth month inside
the most secure of prisoners
our world considered another war.
While you grew, inevitably
so did the danger,
while you swam lazy strokes
in your indoor pool

maybe sucked your thumb
diplomats danced decadent steps
soldiers massed east of here
the media were in overdrive.
Not many noticed
but you took part in the protest
your silent presence

adding weight to the pleas
for peaceful solutions.
In those moments
I clung to the thought of you
a flower in the desert,
though I did wonder if you'd
better stay indoors.

COPYCAT

I've decided to copy the cat:
lie full-length on the carpet
admire
my physical features
indulge
an affectionate stance
toward hair and skin
licking at
dirt, salt and daily smells
till my surfaces gleam.

I'll trim my toenails
with my teeth
nibble irritating lumps
rub with saliva'd hands
behind ears
and over nose
lift a leg for close inspection
caress into smoothness
the stomach
reach further and further
with my tongue
smiling that cat's smug smile.

Meanwhile
I'll work on the purring, too
learn in didgeridoo-style
continuous breathing.

HEALING HAT

The grey wool beret
makes too bald a statement,
as a concealer
of chemo hair-loss;
I turn for answers
to Grandma's button-box,

tumble out a shoal of brightness,
rainbow fish flickering
around a coral reef,
jaunty reminders
of family narratives,
some eyes filled
by fading threads
of sadness.

As I stitch on
my mixed haul of buttons,
each one persuades me
that it will hold things together,
knows what to do
if ever in a hole.

I trawl the heap again for one
to fill the last space –
a tiny, silver horse-shoe surfaces,
the final touch of luck.

SPROUTS

First eaten in ancient Rome
these cousins of the cabbage
spiralling sturdy stalks
like green rosebuds,
keep their secret
curled
in overlapping leaves,
till at their most
post-frost sweetness
they are caught
in supermarket nets
for the Christmas table.

'Crucified' at the base
plunged
into boiling water –
but wait -
sprouts are more delicate
than their dense sphere suggests,
if overcooked
they will release
their hidden weapon
a sulphurous odour –
the Devil
is in the detail.

RARE ORCHID

*The Paph Sanderianum orchid, known as the
Jungle Warrior, blooms only once in a decade.*

After a day of fuses and sockets
the electrician retreats each evening
to his greenhouse's humid embrace.
His dynamic protégées
flaunt their frilly skirts
flash freckled tongues
between glossy lips
luminous wings sparking
magenta, yellow and white
into the gloom.

He moves shyly among them
speaks softly
of light, time, beauty
and inevitable fading.

Every night of this tenth year
a last check on his 'jungle warrior':
and the torch-beam reveals
one elongated bud has just split
exposing a coil of red ribbons.

Days later
a neighbour finds him
earthed on a dark bed
his pale face lit with eternal joy
crimson tendrils wired
into the shock of white hair
like a classical hero.

ON PORPOISE

on the way home
sea flattens into mesh
fifty noses
burst through
pursued by grey pod-bodies
in wet-mac look
thrashed aloft by cleft tails
unleashed Zeppelins
inflated by millennia of certainty
arching
twisting
exuberant children flopping

then streaking the surface
flipper to joyous flipper
challenging the engine's throb
Olympians surging to the tape
losers shattering our wash
into frosted glass

purposeless porpoises
infectious as laughter
sharing air
but not our anxiety
offering moments
free of fear
of shrinking ice-caps
then fins briefly doffed
they melt away

FALLING STAR
On seeing CCTV footage of the last train journey by Annelli Alderton, found murdered in Suffolk woods, December 2006

Like an extinguished star
travelling to earth
for repeated dying
frail being of the night
flutters in a bright box

luna moth skitters
against a lampshade
alights briefly on a seat
wriggles free of its warmth
flits again to a window

moon face with cratered eyes
lips, still tasting son's kiss
moue at the black mirror
craving a spoon of snow
seared by naked flame

she fingers blonde wisps
at the restless nape
hitches up her shoulder-bag
drifts towards a door
turns to check the rear view

drawn again to the seat
drops heavily
shrugs off the bag
gazes at her translucent ghost
etched on passing darkness

luminous vulnerability
wings towards its predator
with tragic insouciance
our aching sadness of hindsight
unknown to night's stars

MICKEY v. MINNIE

Playing Mickey Mouse
at primary school
was my first taste of performance -
classmate, Charmian Wells,
a beauty with perfect features
and glossy, black hair,
inevitably cast
as glamorous Minnie.

For reasons I no longer remember
we rehearsed in a puddle
of mutual dislike.
No question my partner bagged 'cute' -
in red and white polka-dot dress
giant matching bow
on top of her head.

I didn't mind her being prettier than me
because I was funnier.
But she thought so, too.

Moments before our entrance,
grabbing Mickey's wired tail
in Minnie's oversize, white gloves,
she put a large kink in it.

Too much the *ingénue*
to exploit this new feature,
I blushed
the colour of Mickey's shorts.

But I've always said
that bent tail set me
on a theatrical learning curve.

BURNING PRIMROSE

For three weeks Primrose was mine:
my first car
a yellow Ford Anglia
poor starter, but my pride
until one foggy night.

Dawn, I'm called from bed
to find her sagged in the gutter,
flames of lust licking a peeled shell,
steering-wheel buckled,
seat-frames spewing springs
like silver guts,
a tilted wing-mirror
violation's lone witness.

The fire-engine came hot-foot
from similar blazes - four in all.

Over steaming mugs police confided
they knew the culprit,
left prison the day before
with pyromaniacal form.
Had his hot prints all over it
you might say.

But psychology was not their concern -
my questions about deprivation
childhood abuse,
or failed driving tests,
and possible therapy
fell on helmeted ears.

And I'll never know if he had the joy
of watching Primrose burn.

DEAD SISTER'S GLOVES

The apartment door resists my push
then cold air strikes
but the Christmas Tree
winks warmly.

Hall table - beside the phone
flashing a message -
her black leather gloves
Gucci, of course,
curled like her fingers
pleading -
a life melted into a tufa model
of her hands.

Dabs of wrist perfume
linger
on the gloves.

I see again those hands:
the right holding aloft
yet another cigarette,
the left sketching a figure
with spare lines
that instantly come alive.

Finger by finger
I reverse her action,
pull on the gloves,
feel her touch.

SOLSTICE
*Halcyon Days (from alkyonis, Greek for kingfisher)
usually occur around the winter solstice*

Late winter afternoon
harbour water soothed
into glass
a few weathered boats nudging
sun ebbs away behind mountains
that meander
into mournful mauveness.

As I turn for home
a kingfisher streaks along the harbour edge,
a sapphire spark
in a cold, grey world,
he twists
catching light
like a flash of inspiration
then off to spear a fish.

I peer into gathering gloom
greedy for a second share
of such exuberance
and he returns,
swift as a gasp of pleasure,
empty-beaked
yet bearing his blue iridescence of hope,
red-breasted confidence,
white ear-feathers for peace –
or maybe just the brief respite
of some halcyon days.

ALIVE, ALIVE, OH!
*Twenty Chinese cockle-pickers drowned
in Morecambe Bay, February 5, 2004*

A cold coming they had,
trafficked as cargo,
boxed like stinking fish,
hooked by the bait of betterment,
gilled in a snakehead net of debt,
forsaking Fujian beaches
in hope of other shoals to fry.

A cold arriving they had,
in Lancashire winter, to trade
their humid, southern coast
for northern, windswept shores.
Delivered to a sea of mattresses,
no heat, no taste of Oolong tea
to warm the heart's cockles.

A cold living they had,
slave-driven to the daily harvest,
panning icy water for grey and gold
molluscs, curled in pearly beds,
ribbed shells grinding into bags,
Chinese faces bent over, foreign
ghosts in a bleak expanse of bay.

A cold dying they had,
sky faded in the west, dark wading
in treacherous mud sucking at boots,
swirled past tractor tracks to safety,
no asylum from the racing tide,
ears drowned in the music
of sweet Molly Malone.

AFGHAN COAT

In the heady days
of flower power
and all you need is love,
I prized my Afghan coat,
its bright threads rambling

on dark hide,
lined with grey tangles of wool
from hardy mountain sheep,
whose stench assaulted
passersby
when I wore it in the rain.

Not sure I knew then
where Afghanistan was.
Now its images scar
my inner eye:
straggling poor
in medieval layers

dusty turbans
topping Kalashnikovs
names of Kabul, Kandahar, Tora Bora
echoing in my head.
And the coat? Lost
with all my presumed innocence.

MATTER

our cosmic importance is illusion
like stars, we are all only matter
god is a dark matter of delusion
our cosmic importance an illusion
we're dust-specks, in conclusion
significance is just human chatter
any cosmic importance an illusion
like stars, we are all only matter

FIRST BALLET DRESS

Unsmiling
the five year old poses
before studio drapes
in her mother-made tutu
satin bodice soft as skin.

Her pleasure in the swell of tulle,
spinning round on pink pumps
cross-ribboned
over white ankle-socks,
subdued for the camera's click.

The right foot points
offering the promise of dance,
thumbs and forefingers
lift skirt edges toward flight,
long hair woven into the plaits
so loved by her late brother.

Photograph of a dream dress
to erase nightmares
of an accident.

FALL OF A SPARROW

A magpie shrieks a warning
from a branch of the eucalyptus,
as a player drives a yellow ball
over the taut net,
racquet strings sing
when the ball strikes
then soars
and a sparrow in the flight-path
drops
as if felled by a hawk.

I slide my fingers
under the near weightless body,
hoping to feel life's tiny throb,
but her head lolls on a broken neck
one barred wing feathers across my palm
scaly feet dangle from a doll's pink legs
the open eyes are blank
as on a marble statue.

Somewhere a partner waits, perhaps,
or her nestlings
raise their expectant beaks,
but there was no special providence
for this sparrow.

What were the odds of that collision -
the chances of that particular fracture
between life and death?
We all face such possibilities -
moments of unreadiness
for leaving an infinitesimal space
in the universe.
And who will note our fall?

GOLDEN RULE

In a forgotten drawer
my father's wooden rule,
brass-hinged to unfold
sideways and lengthways
for measuring boat timbers.

I hear the slap and click
of its closing,
before I can say 'lifeboat',
see it vanish
into that long pocket
on the thigh of blue overalls.

Indicator of his precision
love of numbers
a life measured
in feet and inches
business takings
cricket scores
football pools
bingo calls.

His emotions kept in check,
marked off by pencil,
held in columns,
buttoned up in cardigans,
till an outburst
a sea-squall soon past.

Now he's gone
to talk spans and cubits
and dead-reckoning
with Noah.

III : TRAVELLER TALES

IN THE MIST

Higher up
recent rain muddies the climb,
slim bamboos cluster.
Then they are there
a gentle group
crouching between trunks.

Curious eyes wide
teeth bared
gestures so like ours.
98% DNA in common
we took different paths
through the forest
way back.

Some grip heavy sticks
blend with the leaves
others lean forward eager.
Some youngster stands
on her head,
a male rolls over
his Buddha stomach.

Two females swing from one arm
like jungle commuters
till everyone hoots.
After an hour
they disappear into mist.
Our chief silverback farts and says:
Those humans are well habituated.

COMET OVER LESOTHO

Pony-trekkers gather
in the stable-yard's velvet dark,
round-topped mountains
circle
like a gem-filled crown
reflected in night's canopy.

Fingers point -
a bright sphere trails a glowing tail
sharp as a disco laser-beam,
carves a purposeful arc
drawing us
into the wake
of softly spinning stars.

Our host whispers
into breath-held silence:
*My daughter just told me
she's pregnant.*

In the pause
a pony whinnies,
then someone remarks:
A comet is an auspicious sign.
No-one laughs.

TO THE CAMEL

Quadruped ruminant
marvel of adaptation:
filmstar lashes
and self-closing nostrils
to baffle dust-devils
leather tongue to subdue thorns
fat-storing hump
triple folding hind legs
(with ready-calloused knees)
cushioned, floating feet.

For this Rajasthani model
the last straw is a long way off.
Unlike Middle Eastern relatives
(obstinate, vicious complainants)
yours is a gentle disposition
for carrying packs, pulling carts
decorated marching in camelcades
even dancing at fairs: like a cobra
neck and head tilted back
front legs prancing to ankle-bell music.

You sail imitation oceans:
sands rippled by a tideless wind
over dune waves, timeless grains
susurrating through two-toed feet
that slipper across a hushed landscape
where (as at sea) distance deceives.
You tilt your snooty nose
at the setting sun
a lofty god, who has no truck
with the eye of a needle.

AMAZON GREEN

vibrant verdancy
greener
than a parrot's wing
brushes rainclouds
bruised with beryl

jade umbrellas
of spreading cedar
arch over olive, fronded palms

emerald moss
rampant on giant gum
subdues ferns
in feathered aquamarine

viridian vine joins sage strangler-fig
to thread warps and wefts
of leaf tapestry
woven with blushing orchid
sapphire butterfly
dancing hummingbird
and scarlet macaws
rehearsing harsh dialogue

swollen waters swirl
skirt towering trunks with silver
an unblemished mirror
doubles the lush forest
deceives the envious eye
beginningless
endless
world of dreaming boughs

sudden opal drops of rain
shatter reflections
each tree shudders
as if loggers have come

VISITING LA

Hotel Roosevelt's deco splendour
lingers
on star-studded boulevards
that overtake the famous footprints
outside Mann's Chinese Theatre.

Neon ribbons highlight
unreality here
where the air is heavy with optimism:
today a waitress
tomorrow a film-star.

Posturing villas
announce Beverly Hills
each superimposed on a neighbour
boasting fake stones
and false pillars.

Above it all, LA's Coliseum
the Getty Centre
stretches like a pale lion
in fossil-filled stone carried
from Rome
in a hundred ships.

Artfully displayed treasures
glow here
true riches
of the European mind,
not celluloid deceptions.

DRIVING THROUGH BUTTERFLIES

In a faraway red curve,
spiked by camelthorn trees,
sky and desert meet.
I swerve the car to avoid
a *corps de ballet* of butterflies
on tiptoe across the dirt road,
tattooed saffrons thrusting tongues
into darkened sand,
a cloud of wide-eyed tortoiseshells
powdering the windscreen brown.

A lull in the winged deluge
lets the Namibian sky astonish –
its silver shoals dart
between layers of aquamarine,
creamy swathes slide together
smooth as Japanese screens,
and umber silk in shreds
unveils puffballs of steam
that dissolve like the last whispers
of a dying breath.

I drive in a dream
towards tear-laden vapour,
that brews up thunderous bruises,
pierced by synaptic lightning,
while orange crystalline shapes
open and close their gauzy wings,
like butterflies,
harbingers of brief joy
and sudden death,
ghosts under my wheels.

CARETTA CARETTA
(Loggerhead turtle)

Under flint-sharp stars
resolute tracks drag across sand,
guided from distant depths
by an inner magnet
to nest where once she hatched.

Tears grind down leather cheeks,
as she delves darkness,
excavates a surrogate womb
for the necklace of ping-pong balls
glistening beneath her tail.

Flippers scatter grains
to hide her treasure,
she rests,
scatters again wider.

At last, her great shell heaves
to face the beckoning sea,
her maternal mystery untouched
by how few hatchlings survive
the collective scuttle seawards,
or ingesting plastic for jellyfish
or the haul from net to table.

She clambers over rocks,
abandoned by the retreating tide,
melds silently with her element.
And we are the loggerheads.

AT THE FLEADH

Musicians hunch
in a Stone Circle
till heads, fingers, feet
nod, flicker and tap.
A feisty fiddle jaunts
across rippling hills,
the accordion foams
through coastal fingers,
banshee flutes swirl
like morning mist,
the bodhran stamps
its sodden feet on peat
and Celtic vocals soar,
high as a wheeling gull
over Ballybunion's cliffs.
Now a melody sighs
past pastel homes,
raining drumbeats
on steep-pitched roofs,
spins out a fireside tale,
its husky voice growling
through smoky bars
till the circle closes,
sounds softly subsiding
like a pint of Guinness
settling in its glass.

DOWNSTREAM

A dead woman waits
on a bank-side bed, behind her
more patient bodies stack
and willing hands build a pyre.
Her husband and son crouch
with a priest reading prayers
the Ganges lapping their sandalled toes.

Logs piled high are put to the match
black smoke shrouds stokers;
the son casts marigolds on the water,
holds a meagre cloth
above her nakedness
as father cleanses her with sacred drops.

Flames lick fiercely
at the wooden heap
passing boats ride bright ripples
and charred specks spiral onto my hand.

Life here flows openly into death,
no coffin, electric curtain, piped music
but a natural process
of enviable certainty
lighted candles floating
downstream
as laundry wallahs stretch out white cloths
to dry in the sun.

WHALES AT HERMANUS

Grey sea is big with them,
dark shadows glide below
the surface, turn, disappear,
belying their bulk.

Binoculars scan half-moon bay,
white-horsed waves galloping,
watch for V-shaped spouts
as rain smudges the lens

framing this journey's end.
Glistening back breaches,
crusty with dark barnacles,
and a second fin, her baby,

drifts in a sideways current,
too close to the beach, perhaps;
tails thrash, pale bellies roll,
a tiny eye gazes at us on shore.

SANDSTORM

A thumbed pie-crust of sandstone
ripples the skyline,
smooth hips and dimpled flanks
of dune-sculpts sunbathe
then in a quiet wind they start to smoke.

Round a scoop of emerald water
oasis palm-trees turn belly-dancers
arms flung above startled skirts
deep hollows whip-lashed
into boiling cauldrons
a world changing contours
4WD tracks instantly erased
as we creep forward
grains spiral against the windscreen
nil visibility
wheels spinning
engine furious
a sliding figure of eight etched
as we attack the ascent.

Through the dark veil
a faceless Touareg
tall on his white camel
that sways on knobbly legs
overtakes our Toyota
floats up the slope
fades as if rubbed out.

FEET OF CLAY
On seeing the terracotta warriors in Xian

They return my gaze
as if just brought to attention,
rank upon unending rank, wrought
from an emperor's fear of death.

Bright colours faded to terracotta
dust from dust
yet life's individual pulse
in a personal topknot twist
angle of hat
length of tunic.

Under closer inspection
they resolve into other armies,
re-assembled from fragments of time,
marching
in unquestioned obedience
to history's echo
of the broadswords' clash,
moustaches barking orders,
goose-steps slapping tarmac.

At the rear, severed heads half-buried,
a hand thrusts through cracked clay
towards a comrade,
a hero's unlimbed torso leaning forward,
eager to rejoin the fray.
But the back of each warrior
reveals his vulnerable nape,
like a child
left to cross the road alone.

GLACIER

Peaks hunch
in an age-locked wilderness
guard its secrets
eagle shadows thermal overhead
seals widen their gaze below

the milky mirror
of her brilliant blue womb
ripples with waterfalls;
might of silt-dusted snow
and pebble-dashed ice

sighs, groans, creeps
imperceptibly,
etching rocks with datelines
of her passing,
till she gives thunderous birth

to sculpts that shimmer
into the bay
past the glide of my kayak
a speck of flotsam
lured on

by crystal flurries;
silence drowns all,
the world is on hold -
I am caught
like a flaw in sapphire

TIGERHUNT

The elephant sways
on wrinkled soles
shrugging her body loose
inside its skin,
dragging me through bush.

Suddenly I am an urchin
before the emperor -
he stretches on a sunlit rock
a fur-clad star
unerringly finding the spotlight.

Ebony lines mark liquid gold
like bars of a cage
yet his huge head, proudly free
tilts back to release a yawn,
the eye-aching white of his throat
a flash of Himalayan snow.

He licks between giant claws,
another yawn bristles pristine whiskers.
Then he slides silently
past nervous elephant knees,
his coat flowing
smooth as molasses.

Dry twigs harmonize with stripes
sun-dappled leaves blend
into golden hair
and he disappears
gently erased
like the Cheshire Cat
the white dots backing his ears
vanish
last

KNITTING ENSEMBLE
charango = Peruvian instrument like a mandolin

a tilt of bowlers skeins wool in Cuzco
ponchos squat or rest on Inca stones
rhythmic fingers wind alpaca softness
needle-clicks counterpoint the gossip

ponchos squat or rest on Inca stones
yarn is plucked like a charango's strings
needle-clicks counterpoint the gossip
two beats' pause to reverse the knitting

yarn is plucked like a charango's strings
bright threads hum past a drone of beige
two beats' pause to reverse the knitting
purl one, slip a stitch goes the refrain

bright threads hum past a drone of beige
patterned borders syncopate the plain
purl one, slip a stitch goes the refrain
a cadence of panpipes for casting-off

patterned borders syncopate the plain
rhythmic fingers wind alpaca softness
a cadence of panpipes for casting-off
a tilt of bowlers skeins wool in Cuzco

PRISONER 46664

Mandela's cell
for eighteen years:
three paces by two,
high bar shadows
trap
on the concrete floor
his folded blanket
slop-bucket
tin plate
and mug,
a still-life.

The guide tells
of whites' daily
pettiness,
then with pride:
This was our university,
we learned to read and write,
using secret scraps.

On his sheened cheek
a solitary tear.

FRIGATE BIRD

Sailors' bad omen glides over
never *on* water,
chevrons adjust
with a single, feathery tilt,
ink smudges the breast of snow,
courtship blaze
a razor-cut on its throat.

His aeronautic climb
chalks vapour-trails on Belize blue,
while a shoe-button eye watches
for another bird to rob of its catch.

As he silhouettes in thin air,
palm-leaves over my head
fracture the flight,
like a child's flicker-book.
I'm six again, tracing seagulls
on a very different sky.

Take that part of me, frigate bird,
to soar past Mayan temples
swallowed by jungle,
freefall towards the volcano's fireball,
hover above the reef's foamy wings,
harbouring flickers of fish.

Perch the child I was
on top the mangroves
to share a frail nest
with your solo chick -
you three need never land.

AT GHANDI'S MONUMENT

Startling
in its simplicity
a vast slab of black granite,
unnamed
releasing
an eternal flame,
honours the still living spirit
in the green heart
of Delhi.

On the stone
a scattering of red blooms
and Ghandi's last words:
Oh, lord!
uttered
as his head lifted
from *Namaste!*
to the assassin.

A Hindu
in a finely cut suit
bows his head to the flame,
draws his thumb
across dust
on the polished surface,
presses it
to his forehead.

TOWNSHIP SCHOOL

A doorway
cut in a freight container
reveals shipshape rows of desks
a cargo of bright-eyed crew
uniformed in pride
confident of learning.

The admiral of this fleet
a local mother
herself untaught
launches her small sailors
across the open sea
reliant on home-drawn charts.

The class comes ashore
to sing for their visitors.
As applause fades
to a warm silence
each child chooses an adult
slips a small hand into a waiting palm.

My partner first grips mine
as though the deck might roll.
We exchange names
then she pulls me inside the metal hold
to inspect her exercise book
a log of effort and encouragement.

One squeeze of fingers
and she is gone
leaving an imprint.

DESERT DANCE

tents float
like fifties ballgowns
on sand pale as talcum-powder

beside a fire's fading glow
two jelabias lounge
dance-hall wallflowers

the mirror-ball moon spins
trails her velvet skirt
in Touareg blue
spangled between swirling folds

on the distant hem
star sequins
sharp as ice
dance intensely
sensing death

before she glides on
a cool glance
into our unzipped tent
turns my prone body
to alabaster -
and a small stone dog
curls at my feet